Dear Family,

What's the best way to help your child love reading?

Find good books like this one to share—and read together!

Here are some tips.

- **Take a "picture walk."** Look at all the pictures before you read. Talk about what you see.

- **Take turns.** Read to your child. Ham it up! Use different voices for different characters, and read with feeling! Then listen as your child reads to you, or explains the story in his or her own words.

- **Point out words as you read.** Help your child notice how letters and sounds go together. Point out unusual or difficult words that your child might not know. Talk about those words and what they mean.

- **Ask questions.** Stop to ask questions as you read. For example: "What do you think will happen next?" "How would you feel if that happened to you?"

- **Read every day.** Good stories are worth reading more than once! Read signs, labels, and even cereal boxes with your child. Visit the library to take out more books. And look for other JUST FOR YOU! BOOKS you and your child can share!

The Editors

For all the children
who can write themselves
into this story –NG

To my brother, John Joseph Calvin Lee,
with thanks and love
–NT

▲▲▲▲▲▲▲▲▲▲▲▲▲▲▲▲▲▲

Text copyright © 2004 by Nikki Grimes.

Illustrations copyright © 2004 by Nicole Tadgell.

Produced for Scholastic by COLOR-BRIDGE BOOKS, LLC, Brooklyn, NY

All rights reserved. Published by SCHOLASTIC INC.

JUST FOR YOU! is a registered trademark of Scholastic Inc.

Library of Congress Cataloging-in-Publication Data

Grimes, Nikki
    A day with daddy / by Nikki Grimes ; illustrated by Nicole Tadgell.
      p. cm.—(Just for you! Level 2)
    Summary: A boy enjoys every moment of a special day with his father, as they play in the park, share French fries, and see a movie together. Includes activity ideas for parents and children.
    ISBN 0-439-56850-1 (pbk.)
    [Fathers and Sons—Fiction. 2. Divorce—Fiction. 3. African Americans—Fiction.]
    I.Tadgell, Nicole, 1969- ill. II. Title. III. Series.

PZ7.G88429Day 2004
[E]—dc22

2004042909

10 9 8 7 6 5 4   06 07 08

Printed in the U.S.A. 23 • First Scholastic Printing, February 2004

A Day With Daddy

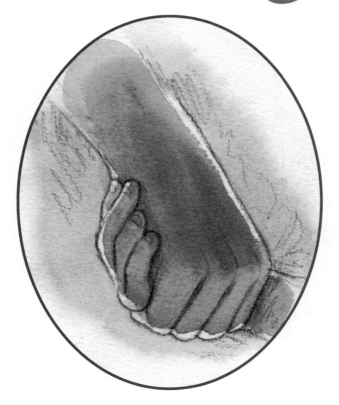

by Nikki Grimes
Illustrated by Nicole Tadgell

Daddy comes for me
soon as the sun
kisses my window.

Mom waves goodbye
when I tell her
I'm too big for kisses.

We bop to the park.
When we get there,
we race
to the basketball court.

We play a game
of one-on-one.
By the time I'm done
sinking baskets,
Daddy is through with me.

"I give up," he cries.
"You are clearly the best.
Whew, boy! Your old
man needs a rest."

I laugh and give him
a minute to breathe.
Then I get an idea.

"Let's speed down the slide
the way we used to
when I was a kid."
So we do.

Next, we soar
on the swings.
Daddy pushes me
until my toes
scrape the clouds.

I close my eyes
and dream
that we are like this, always.
Together.

Later, we join friends
for a little game
of baseball.

Suddenly, my tummy rumbles
and Daddy hears it.
"Want some lunch?"

We go for burgers and fries.
I munch mine slowly
so the afternoon
will last forever.

When we're done,
it's time for a movie
about ninjas,
with lots of karate!
We love this stuff!

Too soon,
the movie ends.

Daddy takes me home.

Now it's his turn
to wave goodbye.
But I'm only a little sad
because we had a great day,
and I know
I'll see him again.

"See you later," I say.

Then I slip inside
our apartment
where I let my mom
give me a hug
and a messy kiss
since she missed me.

That night, I go to sleep, smiling.
I've got enough happy
to last me one week,
which is right about when
Daddy comes again!

Here are some fun things for you to do.

Can YOU Race?

The boy in this story has a special day.
He uses some special words, too!
He says that he and his daddy **race**.
What does that mean?
Can YOU race?
Act it out!

He says, "I **munch** . . ."
What does that mean?
What do YOU like to munch?
Act it out!

Read the story again. Look for more interesting words. Act them out, too!

A Day for YOU!

Plan your own special day. What would YOU want to do?

Make a list of three things.

Will you be with friends or family?

Where will you go?

▲▲▲▲TOGETHER TIME ▲▲▲▲

Make some time to share ideas about the story with your young reader! Here are some activities you can try. There are no right or wrong answers.

Think About It: Ask your child, "Why do you think this is such a special day for the boy in the story? Which part of the story did you like best? Why?"

Talk About It: The author of this story is a poet. Sometimes, poets use words in surprising ways! Ask your child, "What is happening when 'the sun kisses' the boy's window? What do you think is happening when his 'toes scrape the clouds'?"

Read More: Read page 32 aloud to your child. Talk about the author and why she wrote this story. Then visit the library to find more books by Nikki Grimes.

Meet the Author

Photo by Steve Elliott

NIKKI GRIMES says, "Like most children of divorce, I lived with one parent and had limited visits with the other. I consider myself fortunate to have spent as much time with my father as I did, and that time was always special. I looked forward to it, perhaps because it was so rare. Every moment counted and is forever etched into my memory. I think that's true for the boy in my story and for most children in the same circumstance."

Nikki Grimes was born and raised in New York City. She began composing verse at the age of six and has been writing ever since. She is the author of many award-winning books for children and young adults, including *Talkin' About Bessie* and *Wild, Wild Hair*. In her spare time, Nikki likes to make wearable-art garments, beaded jewelry, and hand-made cards. Ms. Grimes lives in Corona, California.

Meet the Artist

NICOLE TADGELL says, "As a child, I spent many hours at the local libraries. Mostly, I had my nose buried in a book, and I never really "grew up" inside. I think I became an illustrator so that I could make books that I wished I could have read when I was young. I had fun using my brother as the model for Daddy in this book. I also really liked using strong spring sunshine for the cheerful, father-son day of fun. And I had a great time swinging on the swings in the park, too. I guess I'll never be too big for that!"

Nicole grew up on Long Island, New York, graduated from Wheaton College, and now makes her home in Spencer, Massachusetts, with her husband Mark and two border terriers. Nicole is also the illustrator of *Fatuma's New Cloth* by Leslie Bulion, the Joe Joe in the City series by Jean Alicia Elster, and *Moving Day Surprise* by Tina Stohlberg.